A SERIES OF SMALL BOXES

Thomas Devaney

ALSO BY THOMAS DEVANEY

POETRY
The American Pragmatist Fell in Love
(Banshee Press, 500 copies)

NONFICTION
Letters to Ernesto Neto
(Germ Folios, 250 copies)

A SERIES OF SMALL BOXES

Thomas Devaney

Fish Drum Inc., New York City   2007

A Series of Small Boxes
© 2007 by Thomas Devaney
Fish Drum books are edited by Suzi Winson
Cover Art: Abbie Winson
Cover and Book Design: Basia Grocholski
Web Macher: Ulrich Leschak
Editorial Assistants: Julie Winson, Mani Tyler, Font LeRoi

FISH DRUM
P.O. Box 966
Murray Hill Station
New York, NY 10156

ISBN 10: 1-929495-11-0
ISBN 13: 978-1-929495-11-5

Library of Congress Control Number: 2007926680
Printed by CDS Publications, USA

To order contact Small Press Distribution
www.spdbooks.org

Published by Fish Drum, Inc.
www.fishdrum.com

For L.S. Asekoff & Trevor Winkfield

ACKNOWLEDGMENTS

Grateful acknowledgment to the editors of the magazines in which some of these poems first appeared: *The American Poetry Review, Cross Connect, Fence, The Germ, Jacket, Jubilat, LUNGFULL! Magazine, The Philadelphia Inquirer, The Poetry Project Newsletter, Pom2, Skanky Possum, Tool a Magazine.* Some poems were translated into French by Olivier Brossard and Yan Brailowsky, and published in the following journals: *Arsenal, Double Change,* and *Poesie.*

"The Car, a Window, and World War II" appeared in the anthology *Walt Whitman hom(m)age* 2005/1855, Eds. Eric Arthenot and Olivier Brossard. (Turtle Point Press/Joca Editions: New York/Paris, 2005); the poem first appeared as a broadside published by the Institute of Contemporary Art (Philadelphia) for the exhibit "Springtide," 2005.

"Trying to live as if it were morning," and "A Free-for-All Ends at A.C. Airport," both appeared in the anthology *The Brink: Postmodern Poetry 1965 to Present* from Yeti Press in Kerala, India 2002.

"Sonnet" appeared in the anthology *American Poetry: The Next Generation*, Eds. Gerald Costanzo and Jim Daniels. (Carnegie Mellon Press: Pittsburgh, PA 2000).

"Sonnet" and "Obi-Wan Kenobi" were first published in *The American Pragmatist Fell in Love* (Banshee Press, 1999).

Grateful acknowledgment is made to the following people for their generous support: Olivier Brossard, L.S. Asekoff, Trevor Winkfield, John Ashbery, Al Filreis, Ingrid Schaffner, Ted Casterline, Gregory Djanikian, Elizabeth Scanlon, John Timpane, Max Apple, Jay Kirk, Francis Ryan, Clement Coleman, hassen, Sparrow, Dean Dakerko, and Zoe Strauss.

Thanks to Ted Casterline for the first two lines of "persimmons to eat and wear as jewelry" section of "Origami Headphones."

Thanks to the MacDowell Colony.

Special thanks to Fish Drum publisher, friend and radiant frequent flyer Suzi Winson.

Last, much love and thanks to Emily Missner, and to my parents Maureen and Tom Devaney.

CONTENTS

A SERIES OF SMALL BOXES

Rome

There are lines from movies
That can ruin your life, is a line,
You say, that could ruin your life.
But was your life already ruined,
Or a ruin like Rome? *Ashes, grass*
And a see-through gown.
I've already ruined enough lines
Not to get this one right.
Yet I've always loved Rome,
The name, that is, not the city,
Which I also love in a way one can love
A city one has loved and been loved in
Because it enters you, in a way, as you walk,
Buy stamps, tell time.
No, for me that isn't Rome,
That is Roma, ages ago, and forgotten.
Or studied and false, though
Comprehensive seeming, a compendium
Of soft brassy light on that providential stone.
But never the single syllable
Swallowed whole, nor its multi-syllabic twins:
Forcible Romulus, clandestine Remus—
Ruinous Rome.

The Car, a Window, and World War II

after Troy Brauntuch

We grew up facing the despised backside of
        an otherwise honest house.
As in all good tales, it is a Period without a period.
The atmosphere in which shirts were stacked
in a Chinese laundry and now live on in us
        like an ancient fern.
Forget forgetting; we depend upon the pin stripes.
Memory calls and says, Shut the window,
        we're CLOSED!
A pledge of discretion, I guess it's a yes or no thing.
The way the remains of an intractable fact remains:
some furs are fake, some are not; a true blond
        poofy hairlet;
the more obscure hood of a car (not a place to sit).
I can't remember all of them that well.

A car is an object like a small country.
World War II: The Palindrome War, WWII.
Mom, Dad, car, window, the never ending WWII.
Das Boot, Enemy At The Gates, Sink the Bismarck,
        To Hell And Back, A Bridge Too Far,
to name but the most memorable Memorials.
First Blood, Drugstore Cowboy, The Terminator,
        Blade Runner—everything on video and
                DVD forever.
To go the distance is not to close the distance.
It's an inside/outside problem.

Once, after the war he shot his gun into a pond,
the dead fish soon rose to the surface.
I could see he could see it, but that's all I could see.
Not another one of his fish stories; he told me once and never
        mentioned the fish, pond, or gun again.

Five inscrutable fingers rest gently against the glass,
        the darkness, the page.
What becomes of a hand in a window,
the shadows cast by a magic lantern, a simple fire?

Losing track of images, losing track of people—
the secret destiny of HDTV on HDTV.

The experimental film *Walt Whitman Nurse and Poet,*
it's not bad; we enjoyed the catalogue of birds.
The dull and unmusical notes of the Yellow-billed Cuckoo,
like the cow, cow of a young bull-frog repeated eight or ten times
        with increasing rapidity.
The way sounds become words, and words
        can store their sounds, and return back to Sound.
As we learned, some of the birdcalls and songs were recreated
        from written descriptions.

And T, like me, adores the tabby and often says,
"It's not always better to know better."
Ask yourself this question:
Does silence have to mean a lack of sound?
I hate the lack of sound myself, though crave the silence.
Yesterday, three people were shot at a check-point.
The difference between a moment of silence
        and a decade of silence.
A lone piano plays into our daily commute.
Gravel, pretzel bits, a penny on the floor. VACUUM:
        50 Cents.
Sonic Youth behind another pane of glass, glazed.
They didn't invent *flesh as material*, only the name:
        "Adaptation Studies."
The late afternoon light through the painted window
becomes part of the notes on the page.
Trace the tire marks, the fuel leak on the carpet,
        call them "relics."
She was emphatic: "I don't read the quotes, I skip them."
A statement which clearly gave her a lot of satisfaction.
This was years ago, hence the spaces, hence the space.

Deliberate

after Lorenzo Thomas

In the basement of Double Happiness
We sit on our secrets.
The man nearby doesn't nod,
But opens his marked and watery eyes wider.
I take it as hello and it is.
His eyes are older than he is
And he is not so young.
It's how he looks when he looks,
And looks good too.
Sharp and serious, one of the older guys
You say hello to, but never know,
And yet know all the same.
Smoke in the spotlight, he isn't from Philadelphia.
"A good place to be *from*," he says, a plume
In its progress from one end of the darkened room
       to the other.
So he sits;
       then he's up, then he stands
Like our fifty states and minds.
And then we're here, and he says—

But here's the truth:

You have the right to keep your mouth shut

Trust me,

Across the room
A person looking like a crazy version
Of somebody you once knew
Might be our Savior
One who can draw fire
Out of ashes
At least a lover, maybe
The one to take you up a little higher
Or let you down easy.

But don't look this way,

It isn't me

4

In Iceland there's no reason

to mention the giant wave
the ocean falls   the sky
a swell   a dropping edifice three
or more stories   past the brim
barrier walls   there are no problems
the apartments of negative space
have no visitors
the house breaks o'er the coast
green moss o'er the lava hills
the sun is out   for fifteen minutes
makes a fast-reverse   and is out again

William James and the Giant Peach

to J.C. Hallman

James ate the giant peach and waited for the rain.
It wasn't a children's story, but an entire year
      of his journal razored out.
The August heat had taken its toll on the garden.
The clouds hung low over the upstate hills.
It wasn't raining raining, but it looked like rain.
James relaxed his shoulders and walked.
He didn't feel the rain, but could see it falling
Lightly across a field of gentle showers.
You can go to the Adirondacks by yourself.
James recognized the freestone's curve and
Golden natural split. Leaves leave their mark,
The blush is stained amber. The enchanting prints
Of leaf, sun, and skin: radiant and nude.
From James's experience the soul ached.
He laughed at himself, but still couldn't sleep,
Buy a horse, or make up his mind.
In most cases he preferred a mid-size peach.
On hottest day of the hottest month,
It's easy to like a peach, even a giant one.
All mouth, all mind, the plain and high fields
      coalesce and stretch.
Yellow-gold flesh on the turn to golden fruit.
Peach passing into peach.
Taste varies with movement.
From hand to wrist and chin to ground—juice
      and more juice.
James wiped his mouth with his hand,
And hand on his handkerchief.
The red and inborn gift of a fine-grained pit,
Held, loved, and gone too.
A little more mountain and a little less valley
      and light.
Is this what "half" looks like?
Damn the causes, damn the effects.
The universe meets us half way.
When it's perfect, "the perfect peach"
      Is the perfect phrase.
Don't tell, never tell. Valley, mountain,
Sun-behind-the clouds—James never did.

Quick Bear Poem

Was that a bear? The darker part
      of the dark in the trees.
Should we go back, keep going?
Out of the corner of the eye,
      or the eye itself?
It wasn't the "Bears in the Trashcans"
      of the evening news;
nor the darkly handsome one upright and wet,
fishing on Public Television. It is nighttime,
      we are driving.
Black dot vanishing to the black underfur.
The retina is alive to its widest sphere.
How we do and don't chase
      the night's black thunder.
In the sharp and grassy swiftness,
the upper reaches of the canopy whoosh
as nighttime particles swarm in a sudden light,
and other luminous reflectors dot and dart
on the road up ahead.

Sonnet

You know all those sonnets the ones where I said, "I love you," well
This time, I mean it, this time I'm talking about
Your curly hair soaked black from October's frozen rain.
You reading Milton and eating a BLT.
Our up-front lies about being vegetarians,
(Milton's, "I can not praise a cloistered virtue").
More really, all those times we never kept meeting,
Till we finally never met—giving up,
Till bacon, Milton and the rain were all we had.
Admit now I never wrote you sonnets,
And that this probably isn't a sonnet either,
Tho' I'll call it one, and loud skies pour down
   To live on, back-of-the-brain with you,
   Milton, bacon, your face in a year of rain.

A Northern Straight

to Carl Rakosi

You might or might not have to wait
for the purple house across the street
to sink in, or the clean yellow
molded glass of the front door
and this thick blue window.
There is a patient requirement in
the kitchen's old cream.
Paint painted over paint painted over paint.
Of course one side of the window frame
is larger and sunnier than the other.
An old house, an old man,
old cobalt blue bottles—what is old?
The strong light makes you feel
you should know more people.
For a moment you dip back and forth
between the bright green hills
from the plane ride here and *here*;
a half-inch of far-away snow holding.

A Series of Small Boxes

My best advice has always been small boxes.
So we move. Pack your songs, fringe history of television,
kindergarten constructions, extra socks, somehow it all will fit;
and what doesn't you can bring along too, if you'd like.

In the loneliest days one well-chosen box may abide
            and hold us.
To lift, to be lifted by—and even if we never lift a finger
we may preserve in front of these familiar squares.
A shallow silk green box, its lock of hair long gone;
a single-person hand-painted lunch basket
            and the warmth and hunger for its lunches;
a father's watch and cuff links placed to the side
            in a matte leather box;
and a mother's wooden boxes:
only she knows what treasures they contain,
and how much, and for how long.
Preciousness, friends, is a killer, a deadly sin we know,
yet our ephemera often have a hold well beyond their spheres.
There is Rilke's letter on three twigs of heather.
"Right now one of them happens to be lying
on dark blue velvet in an old pen and pencil box.
It's like a fireworks: well, no, it's really like a Persian rug."

Of the famed small boxes there is the Tiffany small box.
Big Tiffany boxes are a delight, but they are only an ad
for the smaller boxes, the smallest finely-tuned
            turquoise boxes.

A small box of chopsticks is a beautiful thing.
These boxes are their own self-contained wisdom.
A transferring, a lifting: separate, select, one piece,
            and then, another.
Between plate and mouth you can have civilization.

Big boxes cast big shadows, but let's be clear:
big boxes are not the opposite of small boxes.

These boat-sized boxes have their place
        in the real estate of the world.
There is no getting around them, and why should we?
As the great tumbling of childhood goes
nothing's better than a great big box to beat around in.
But how big were those boxes really?
Those refrigerator boxes of youth?
They were huge—and will always remain huge.
I will not speak against their corrugated magic.
They tower over us.
Big boxes fill enough space, yet in a world held together
        by a network of all-dominating boxes
small boxes stack up to their biggest brothers.

A thousand figures, a thousand forgotten figures:
my matchboxes have cost me nothing and little space,
tossed and scattered in a shoe box now doing their tiny
and generous best to hold what might have been, or was.

Small boxes are nested in a nation of monumental boxes.
Still the sadness of so many small boxes arrayed before us
goes without saying (poems, old records, books).
Heavy things are heavy enough, yet to heap and assemble
        again and again is work enough.
Our burnished heirlooms may only cohere
right at this moment, or at a distance, or not at all;
        we do not know.
Boxes of photos in black albums and loose in piles.
Lake Arianna in its panoramic boxes.
Blowing kisses or eating lemons?
Your colorful boxes of *you* taken by *you*.

The Russian composer's English is limited,
but fielding a question she gestures like a dream
to show the peaks and the rolling valleys of Mahler.
Mahler transported for generations
in so many submersible boxes, which are still en route.

And wasted space, the great wasted spaces we know about,
but have only partly charted; as sturdy caskets
        and gilded urns are simply fitting spaces too.
We don't know if "No one really knows." We don't know that.
For us, it's only countless boxes and trying.
A series of hand-made boxes set free from hands and boxes.
A voice within the grain of the wood: an ache released,
        an ache sustained.
Small boxes of sudden joy and sudden unimaginable loss.
The microscopic boxes of supernatural powers collected
over time and which one day arrives; is opened
and then gone, right out the numinous window.

The 1,000-Year Storm

to Emily Missner

The basement wall is not a wall
Only stones soaked through.
Sheets of rain and sheets and blankets,
Your eyes softer and softer.
Water streams under the French doors
            on the basement floor.
A $1,000 deductible—
            for the 1,000-year storm.
All reports are arranged to float or sink,
Cars not stuck near Gladwyne, float
At Conshohocken; on Midvale
Floodwater sweeps woman under;
The sound of water, a truck parked nearby.
Double-crossed at Trenton, boats
            are ordered to moor;
Washington's Reenactors revolt.
Not a drizzle nor merely a downpour—
It's *that* kind of rain.
Hold the space, take their place,
Clouds replace the clouds.

Arriving

In the old days, people
would have to say it.

There would be a big-up
to Coco Chanel.

The question of who's
remaking whom's
Image
might or might not be worked out later.

Everything
from the face
to shoes would be shining
directly so the city
would not forget.

Inevitably there would be talk
of inevitability—
but *talk* all the same.

Heaps of crosswords HERE.

Endless interiors, views, eyes.

The worst of winter would be mild.

Obi-Wan Kenobi

to Ted Casterline

Toward the end of his life Obi-Wan Kenobi
was like an old cat.
He was like, *cut the pomp and circumstance
        and show me the couch.*
The rebels had gone off without him,
his planet a backwater of the known worlds.
It was hard enough to do the little things:
get a decent hair cut, mend his sandals.
He understood longer than he'd like to remember,
that it's the little things, comfortable shoes,
a good haircut, that really keep you going.
And in another hundred and twenty years,
        if anyone remembered,
he didn't want to be known as the "long-haired,
broken-sandaled Kenobi."

A hundred and twenty years of tough love
can put some ideas into your head.
Sure, he could have as much sky as there is to take,
but he's not above the petty:
The pens and pencils of existence, as he calls them.
He makes the Red juice from concentrate
and drinks it all morning,
Says his "May the force be with you," old man prayers.
Then back to his pens, pencils,
faintly ignorant of the window, and the others, thinking,
the old giants can't turn their ships around fast enough.
Today, the pang of a long-gone love's swarmed over him,
invisible, like sand ants on a crater.
Today he notices his sandals, made of Taun-taun,
        or possibly even Bantha,
are beat and in great need of mending.
He'll get them mended, it's a half day's journey.
He'll take leave, traveling light;
the sand ants are clambering in song and dance.

Otherwise

after Joanne Kyger

I get people and the extractive industries confused.
        Everything
            from steel
to Chinese bras.

She says:
      My Lord
          take me to the voice
and let it float.

Float to the bottom
      and stay there.
           Surrounded by silent trees for months,
The voice is deep,

the eyes are closed.
      The smoky sunglasses
          are what take you.
Past the fear of life's paucity,

You might anticipate that *patience,*
        or crazy quilt
           would be the word.
Where else can you be both beautiful and warm?

White is white,
        it takes up space.

Crumb-stained spicy salt between the pages.

Trying to live as if it were morning
to Greg Fuchs

Every character in Dostoevsky is going to be in the hospital
        after this poem.
The underground man with a baseball bat, clearing house
"Philly-Style," and from what I've seen
        it would be true.

I put the Brothers K and their endless array of calamities
        out with my pinky.

I don't go in for the ping-pong of rational-irrational,
        possible-impossible—
The sad, lucid, mad, attractive, murky
        and yes, horrible overcoat of Paradox, Pennsylvania.

I don't need that.

The Bros. K are gone.
The problem of fake hamburger or even real hamburger remains.

The Past at my back,
Back in the past, I agree with John Coltrane
        when he says, "War begets war."

I drive all around my neighborhood with "the Idiot"
        in the front basket of my bike.
When he falls out we pick him up and keep going.
He's clever in a way that any other person might be killed for.

Of course, people don't fuck with us.

It's the old game of imposing order where there isn't any
        then calling yourself on it.

The ancients called it gravity; the modernists, job security.
The people after lost a lot of weight and went home pissed off
Not believing they were home when they actually were,
        so they never really slept.

It's the kind of trouble a fleet of blimps "up in flames"
Might cause flying over an Olympic stadium as seen
        on video cassette—
                but really real anyway, like on fire.

People point out the violence I do to my own words,
How uncareful I can be—I duck under their commentary.

My copy of *Crime and Punishment* is under the aloe plant
        all buckled and stained from water.

A man I respect said there hasn't been any "breakthrough work"
        since sometime in the 1930's.
Sometimes for me it would just be breaking things;

Like my uncle's a "good guy," but
The precinct captain pulled his back-up.
He shouldn't be here. We don't talk about it.

Take out a piece of paper and write down:
Man the builder, Man the destroyer, Man the eater
        of donuts, butter cake, and pork buns.

The experimenter says he, or a recombinant
He and She "unsettles all things."
Even though that's cool, I don't unsettle "all things."
I don't have enough time.
There's enough nonsense without that nonsense.

I'm not here to settle that.
I'm here to write a poem because I'm a morning person
        and it's morning.

This is a morning poem.

It's no fun living in the no-fun zone

At his funeral they said he was,
"Never a downer."

It takes a day every day.
They're filming in your area-code.

The Director asked if you'd stand in.
Things are good, people are over.

Drama, drama, drama, drama.
Grow angry, proofread slop. Lose days.

The specific emotional quality of former sex.
Know the cat knows.

Tomorrow on Oprah will be called:
Creating Damage.

Soup tastes better the second day.
Phone up the hotel. There isn't a job.

All the same, there's no more time.
Go to where you feel a river.

Scan in the ocean.
Remember what you once thought.

You were wrong.
It's not dark.

Something's stuck in your gut.
You still need to eat.

miniature miniature golf
after Philip Whalen

I cannot accept miniature golf
And I refuse not to play,
Or let you stop me from playing.

The bonsai tree lives, the old Huffy bike,
My Citizen's watch, this plasma screen.
I will not leave.

The drawbridge is up
The gate is down. A genius kid
In seven states, ridiculed in the rest.

Oh Wildwood, New Jersey—
Oh Seaside Heights—
Old Faithful Fountain of Youth!

Along the fault of relation
to Jen Hofer

Coffee milk
Is not a fifty-fifty blend.

Something you knit
Like twiggy wiggy, or

Chitty Chitty Bang Bang.
It's a Rhode Island thing.

Runner-up for the State drink:
Del's frozen lemonade

It's not that it's delicious,
It is—coffee, sugar, milk.

Nourish the morning, stay
The sweet empty night.

Everything else succumbs.
No church wedding,

Nor *Mazel Tov* you can pass
Easily over.

At and Near the Georgia Guidestones

The shaky skinny guy at the catfish pond
(no teeth) threw his little rat dog in.

The pebbles in our shoe made it difficult.
We live in the country, it suits us.

"A lucky penny." "A dirty sidewalk."
"A hardboiled and salted egg in your mouth."
"A star at nighttime."

The song continued longer than it needed
to continue, that was the song.

It wasn't "Your Infinite Spicy Mouth,"
or "The Soft Water Sunset," "Old House,"
"The Bay," the memory sunk
in the fluffy bed. Noises in the pillow.

Signs in the SMAL-MART:

WE NO LONGER TAKE BAD CHECKS
WE STILL REFOLD MAPS

The most incredible thing about the whole thing:
thick pieces of brown bread;
all polished wood and clean; lots of pillows.

The red-rubber face of the goose
that chicken-walked up Mosquito Road.
Cool red turban this old lady wore.
Color of the shirt I liked.

A Free-for-All at A.C. Airport

"The airport parking lot was known as a free-for-all where tow trucks
routinely had to sort out the handiwork, ...often with no discernible
ingress and egress." —Amy S. Rosenberg, The Philadelphia Inquirer

New Jersey is the greatest poem never written.
Not an accident, but constant accidental.

Parking space is the central fact to man born in America.
There are several hundred ways not to understand.

Despite the invitation to excess, in A.C.
no bets are placed on the stay-at-home team, Pomona Nomads.

Directions: 1.) Park and lock your car 2.) Fly to Florida for the
winter 3.) Remember, there's little reason to think *New Jersey* when
you're not there—even if that's where you parked.

Influx is the name of the vapors rising off the cinder fields
meeting the black birds as they wield into night.

No way in; no way out: the forward function
is a maneuver all novice tow truck drivers like to do for you.

Your delight in pattern and repetition is dropped off
to search a dusty field filled with hundreds of towed cars.

Until you actually say it, unscriptability and New Jersey rhyme.
The State's equilibrium is located elsewhere.

The car alarm. The unison HONK. The techno field jam.
The songs Bruce Springsteen will not write anymore.

ORIGAMI HEADPHONES

in twelve sections

severely clear

The funeral business was creepy as it probably still is.
We knew we wouldn't change the world, but had the decency
to embarrass the guilty. Persons in the house were often made
to feel an unspecified levity. Whether it had anything to do with
our fluorescent ceilings flickering one thing and our computers
flickering another you can better tell. It was all in front of us, part
of the articulated body of problems, with dozens of bit parts,
which also broke your heart.

emergency numbers

Dirty waters found us before we found them.
It might sound obvious, but by the time everyone knew,
         there was no one to tell.
Saved from the waste of waters, the secret
and hidden determination of some living
and intelligent nature—ancient waters over the present world.
We distrusted our spigots (the 100-mile meal,
the 100-mile suit, *one hundred miles*) there was no story.
One day everyone was just drinking bottled water.

one idea about terrycloth

Spinning, looming, weaving: a widely felt appreciation
for texture. Linc was in the house on his red rubber seat
listening to headphones, reading a magazine. Thought:
finger wagging, pointing on his T-shirt—*I can't believe,*
I can't, can't, believe the way you acted today!
He was over it, but couldn't get the same emphasis,
so he turned it into a song, a wooly song.

the mysterious humors

In the essay about the bloodied and smear-stained kitchen Santas there is a mini-chapter on "Humor." Humorous people spoke of the serious, and serious people spoke of the serious.

summer favors

There was no way to tan safely.
We asked for the sun and had the sun.
Something to drink, something to eat.
It's true Bartram, the best botanist
in the New World, named a tree
for his friend Ben Franklin.
Hide-and-seek behind the hedge.
A kid, a brilliant kid squatting
clumsily out of breath.
Someone said the day would end
in a ten pound bag of charcoal.
Some in seven 2 lbs. bags of ice.
The afternoon was too sunny to last
for more than the afternoon.

dog people

Grandmother's Duke was a Boston Bull Terrier.
Three Dukes in a row were Boston Bulls, and
who needs cloning? Close enough for jazz. No,
they weren't all the same, but neither were we:
and Duke and Duke and Duke.

the old

"Look at those filthy windows. I've got stained glass windows
in my house," the proud woman frowned, shaking
her hands weakly in the air from her chair set in the kitchen.

drop ceiling

Light and dirty as air.
As soon as you walked into the room,
and could think, you thought:
How fast can you get it down?
One way in, one way out:
Head poked up into the dark,
        dusty space.
Lights built into the mix.
Inexplicable wires
        amid the buckled woodwork.
Trashed as it was, you worked towards
the ceiling, holding the ceiling—
wreckage all the way up.

persimmons to eat and wear as jewelry

Bell pushers, leaf-rakers, stump bunnies,
tavern-goers, pebble smokers, and clowns:
Stop all the hair-pulling! It was true
what they always said—they were
"Down with the sickness." But so were we.

why birds don't fly into the glass

Bird watchers had nothing on
      what the birds saw.
The birds were amp-ed
by powers of 10x10. Ornithology
was the public name of Intricacy
      written in the sky.
Augurs never were and never will be
      a metaphor.
They really saw it all: lone moving cars
handmade dresses, views, everything
like this neighboring town below.

the great chain of being

We had a hard time with time.
We weren't the *we* we thought.

A bull's-eye. Brass tacks.
One station shuffling in your ear

((from God to bottomless clod))
A sort of Runic rhyme that welled:

the bells, bells, bells.
We called our cells when we said.

Salad days were the days
we kissed and kissed.

A weird delayed fireworks reaction.
A duet for juggler and harp,

our future twins. Shapes
in all of their shapes

were part of the range.
And all yet to be undone—

all before your eyes.
Your impossible eyes.

roughly fickle activity

A father had died, several were dead.
People stood loosely together.
Their standing was a swerve felt
against other things once felt—
ideas that survive their occasion;
Something physical kept close,
similar to 2000 B.C. when the Japanese king
       had 'flying sun discs' for advisors,
or when Sodom and Gomorrah were plowed under by angels
for not being perverted enough, and Knossos was consumed
for no reason at all. Wind power, bicycles, presence and relative
absence: if you wanted to know a good restaurant,
you could still ask your butcher. A cat and the shadow of the cat.
The weight of the head in the hand remained in the hands.

Near and Far

to John Ashbery

I've never loved a man, woman, or cat.
It's not sad or even a pity, but the greatest thing really.
The most remarkable love poems in the world have nothing to do
     with it.
A man's face, quiet, and skinny-cool body
     in an Italian foreign language class;
The force of a dear woman's mind and body melded
     in a summer yellow dress.
Not a flash in the pan, though that too fills a peripheral need.
It's the impeccable tempo of a friend's question
Opening up to more one-at-a-time questions
     and perfect pauses, taking us
To private far-off places—to here and here again.
The calm, late-night companionship of a book.
Assured in words not to be reassured in words.
No promises past the page only all the moment can hold.
As fast and as slow and as stunning as an eclipse.
On a given moment, about a given moment,
Worthy of a Nobel in Ethics, attending to our attentions.
The weight of a good fork, the small joys of a fine lunch,
     and lunch itself.
Talk-singing the lyrics of "I Got a Gal in Kalamazoo."
The quality of a line related to the next. Again
     and again I fall.
A ballet of attendant parts and wholes: the good, bad,
     lovely, more a *counterpart of what we are.*
Enough for the night, early morning, and a lonesome
     afternoon;
All here before the breakfast crumbs can be wiped
     from the table.
In "If the Birds Knew" I remember you say:
Not only as though the danger did not exist
But as though the birds were in on the secret.
Today the sweltering heat has passed and the wind is soft
     and cool.
Today the wind is not so windy, a perfect morning really.
Not the wind that hit me from all sides in the back of a Jeep
     to Atlantic City a few weeks earlier.

At 80 mph light rain isn't so light.
The unruly wind, straight from central casting,
Is a great stormy friend and capricious local guide.
Drying me off as quickly as clouds cross the highway,
Its contours audible at every swerve: wet hair, dry hair,
        wet air, dry air.
From sea and surf, turnpike, toll, and land:
It's not only glorious dogs who appreciate the charms
        of the wind.
I cup my hands over my ears, let go. Cup. Let go.
Sometimes hold my hand out the side window
        like a child, surf the powerful air. Do it again!
When my friends glance back I break my stoic pose: make a face.
People driving by look twice. I laugh out loud—as loud as I can.
Alone, I breathe in. I realize I am someone else.
        I am somewhere else.
Emily is in the doorway. She proudly translates for the cats:
Explaining: "It wasn't bad of Rupert to wake us up last night.
The kitties said, *No no no—come here, I have something to tell you.*
That mouse was in our house—The House Mouse.
Ru wanted to tell us he did something good for us;
For over thousands of years he was bred to do it!"
I delight in the palpitating tale of last night's caper.
Old windy rumors of instinct and circulation:
A beautiful dead mouse between us, its soft gray fur licked clean.

One Hour, October

The early winter sky, empty and violet
       with one low star.
How unrushed the rush.
A plodding novel remains still
for several pages taking its time,
in the way novels can, to listen
       to the skyscraper
actually swaying in the wind.

A team of engineers worked out the math
fifty-five years ago.
                The paintings
still have to be straightened every morning.
The compression: a clown wearing less
and less make-up till the day the silence
       says your name.
Someone gets on a bus, someone walks away,
it's all off-camera, it's that big.

B. Downing's Shirt Weapon

This morning I found your sonnets.
They don't look like sonnets.
I think you're making it up.
I should read them again before going on
though it's difficult to wait.
Despite the care, when you're here
we won't figure it out any better.
Holes are perfect for making the wallpaper look good,
patterns waxed and unglued.
Using spackle, or spectacle,
might make us more honest.
I want to say *submerged* but not be held to it.
There is plexi-glass
      and a single speaker behind something
             out of view.
The crease wrinkles my world.
I roll the ball on the green before the game,
paint the gallery walls myself—
searching for a spot to hang them out.

The Rat and the Flower Pot
after Brenda Coultas

Under the window the broken pot shards,
cactus, and former spry brown rat.

One floor up you remember
it was a rat who said,

"Nothing is easier
For the mind to know

than itself." Odds
of the squirrel offing

the drunk and still,
out the window sill—

you have not wrestled
until you've wrestled the rat.

People keep their mouths and
windows shut. Like records

when they were *records*
and letters *letters*.

Correctional tape and
typewriters will never write

this story. A lust
for the old lurid

images, gravitational pull
now, not even consulted.

The mechanics of inner space,
the lapse and the rat

and the rat and the flowerpot.
A great and squandered vanity.

Only the amoebas are happy
after Ernesto Neto

Shoes, bracelets, headphones, boots:

everything on the floor,

every thing a pile.

It's difficult to walk right

into the sculpture, the amoeba.

In front of this completely supportless white,

you wade two feet into this brightness

this biomorphic pillow.

Something does, something doesn't hold

its shape.

Your body displaces the place

you land—

beads, spandex, white button habitat.

(In the immense quiet

white sheen—

in the middle of the afternoon

in the middle of the week

in the middle of the blue

you are completely surrounded.)

The Big Bang of bean-bags—

a lot of sewing going on.

Fragile fragile barra-bola. The rambling,

scrambling air-lifting patterns

of the styrofoam beads

spilling out

all-over the poured concrete.

Mr. Glinting as seen off the Atlantic seaboard

In a long line of long lines
I turn the page of Rimbaud's *Illuminations*
And read two stanzas in French before realizing
I'm reading French and I don't read French.

This is your Saturday morning idea of Saturday morning.
You're the blue man: shirt, pants, lunch, eyes —
anything else you can think — it's all blue.
You take little offense to being called "a willing puppet,"
"A corrupted file," or "a sketch quickly drawn."
Giant white, giant blue, and 250 miles of brown
        that can't contain its green
Are good to look at between New York and DC.

A persistence of vision isn't exactly it.
Perhaps what I'm talking about is what you think
While you read this. Not what I'm saying.
But that isn't exactly right either.

Still, there's a frame-by-frame freedom.
A shot. Another shot, in the arm.
(Stainless steel belly of airplane overheard)
Calling the sparkling blue of the Chesapeake "cartoon-like"
        or "cartoony" isn't a put-down.
But last night's gossip won't hold up to this morning's shiny
        marathon.

It's a Saturday that calls for a few answers,
Not a few more questions.
Let's not talk about whether it's safe to live in America.
Your degree in Manipulation Theory
With a concentration in the "calculating wag"
Will work itself out. You'll get paid: we'll cut you a check.

Heaped Up from Hell

Right and right; the tyranny of beautiful eyes.
He continued to serve the Devil.
It was a crime punishable under a 1937 law
          by up to five years imprisonment.
Harum-scarum the walking riot.
The world is clear.
Things are black and white; sneakers and butternut.
You feel his thoughts, savor their opulence.
The sky is blue,
          Egypt and a small wooden desk.
The story is scattered in sturdy old shoes everywhere.
The part people call *romance* shifted the supernatural to his feet,
making much of the mysterious effects of magic, spells,
enchantments: two children in serious talk.
This was his threat.
They told him he would come to a bad end.

No Such Poem

to John Coletti

John, hug "like a quilt truck."
On the roof "Cooing a page
        in the twilight."
Quilts, quilts, quilts: how can I
describe their single-stitch tred?
I know if you knew, you'd take us—
I know that. As you do, and *do*.
You don't say, "You don't say."
Nor I don't want to live like a story.
A translucent brown lanoline floor-dust
is there for you to see, sweep,
blow away, note by slow dusty note.
No bull, yes; "someone stole."
JC enters the ring: it's war, it's peace—
        Leo T. to a *T.*
Ted and Ted G. are in the corner,
        your cut men.
Curly hair Coletti, measured eyes, measured
        lips—the measure of a moan
"Sewn inside your ear" to keep.
The conceit of *this* and all conceits.
All the silent bruises I have ever loved,
the "emotional surface" scratched and gone too.
Wrapped in blankets, no one asking if it's a flood.

A Return to Glory
after Mark Twain

First one hound and then another
Went for the man walking across the field.

Knowing dogs, he stopped,
Faced them, keeping still in their pow-wow.

Like that, a hub of a wheel, spokes
Made out of the dogs,

A circle of fifteen stretched up
And on him, a barking, tackling,

Howling and more a-coming,
Sailing over fences (the field

Coming toward him across the field)
And around corners, from everywheres.

Accurate Clouds

And so you find she left because
she did not like to stand on concrete

for too long. Now you feel the bones
and the painted floor in your shoes.

What did she say again and again,
or only once? "The lace is effaced."

"The lace, effaced." What you say
is what you heard said, not what was

said. As the way you begin to see
those you've seen only once.

When the time comes to twirl her hair
a small finger of red is all that will count.

Outside, the tingle-tangle of the afternoon
streams out before you—

between opposing buildings
and empty spaces—you walk

through the tag and dregs sale,
the sidewalk and the sky.

A T-shirt, paint speckles, a one speed bike;
Another false alarm, and another.

They're fighting in Atlantic City, in Atlantic City

The urge to put question marks after everything.
Counting the loss, magnetically stripped:
    1-800 generally desensitized.
Now that I'm saying this keeping it going isn't proof.
They're fighting in Atlantic City, in Atlantic City.
Legs on a chair, three fingers resting lightly on her shin.
You don't have to get abstract to see everyone's beat-up badly.
It's not the future it's Lunchtime all around.
The many ways you think about shaking off the outfit.
The kindergarten teacher's countdown to silence.
This quiet, this time of day—call it a nap.
The fried salmon burger and the salad were good.
Where did we leave the exclamation points?
The train took me home in twenty minutes, I was grateful.
I don't live anywhere.

Animated Folkies

All the ninjas seem to be landing here.
They must be on break.

You realize you realize you realize
there's something.

It's about time we hear the story of the lucky duck.
My lucky duck.

Great skeins crashing:
kid kid kid.

There's trouble when the old slow furies
start their laughing.

There's trouble and there's *trouble,*
and there's the old slow furies.

The gall of your pretend hero,
eating twenty-eight chicken tacos.

Before the short story class
you never knew that ain't right—

it ain't; and twenty-eight less tacos in the world.
Somehow the string section makes sense.

The occupying ninjas like a house full of cats;
they must live here now.

The film runs along.
And the furies, old and slow.

Jesus Christ, they've still got it.
School is out, time for a love story.

Your best friend says it plain,
says, she can make you happy.

There's no leap nothing will blow these lines.
Kids keep saying regret regret:

Makes me *what* to write a song.
Don't look up.

Ex-large and kindness,
kind of oversized-ness.

Can't get enough of your crazy love.
Blue sky so blue; so big, so blue blue blue.

Boy don't fit the description
Even at night, the spangled blue

surrounding the car frames your face,
totally cheap frames.

Everything else, blown away: rolled down
rolled down your window.

Yeah, I've been there,
there ain't nothing there.

Now where are you, can't hear
a thing in the wind.

Now where are you?
Now where? Fury. Fury.

At the end of the famous catalogue of the ships
to Suzi Winson

Something didn't look right.

The past flipped into present.

Its trick was it wasn't a trick.

Standing in a room happily devoid

Of everything that ever looked right, now

      it was this, it was here.

If you could think at all, you had to think again.

It was a place you wanted to distrust because

      of a familiar smell or because

The fear that can never cross the screen

      just did.

If it was possible to tell you directly I would.

A person you didn't know, but wanted to

Take a walk with, anywhere beautiful would do,

Spoke, and stood when not speaking,

      in a mid-alto range.

It was cold and I had a pocket of sticky figs picked

From a craggy city garden. They were no good to eat.

The skyline had resembled fake art for the past fifty years.

Everything I had to say I didn't need to say.

POEM
to Al Filreis

Even John Cage worked within the limits of his name.
I am only describing something—and that never stopped
Cage from introducing himself.
You have a question for the six-year-olds;
a question for *all-the-same-height* third graders;
a question for the spinning middle school kids
        who also sing.
You have a follow-up question for the one-word answer:
yes, no, Whitman high school students;
and many questions for the *I-like-it, I-don't-like-it*
college students—the college students.
And for openers you problemitize "problemitizing"
        for the graduate students.
And you have a question for the adults
        and many more for yourself.
Or the question you asked me—to gloss
        the Wallace Stevens line:
"Nothing that is not there and the nothing that is."
And where do questions come from—
        and where do they go?
"Nothing + Nothing = Something, that is 'Nothing,'
which is *really* Something," I said not knowing
where that came from. But is it all about the questions?
It's the amplitude you feel, hear, see, and
for the moment—and longer (we hope)—we feel,
        hear, and see too.
I am describing *you* at our limits, that is, our best
        failed distinctions.
As there are suppers and there are *suppers:*
a butterflied fillet of sole resting on its crunchy skin.
And it's not that you grew your beard, but
you never shaved it off, and that it continues to grow.
Your beard in its place is an invisible element
of that place—made visible.
Here is a line for not talking, which isn't silence,
(the privacy of public communion).
Here is a line for braving dark distances on foot.
Here is a line for space and classical amber bees.

And one for all the ones crossed-out.
I am only describing, as words are one way,
        and walking is another.
So cross the street and step out for a walk,
one we will never take again. I am only describing something,
the way the finest grit becomes the sand we love.
And its warm color comes from whatever light there is,
even if there isn't much at all.
And old John Cage doesn't go away—new John Cages
        just get added.
And where, dear John, is where?